My Life as a

'FEMINAZI'

Blog Series

Part 1

By T. Crocker

Some names and identifying details have been changed to protect the privacy of individuals. I have tried to recreate events, locales and conversations from my memories of them. In order to maintain their anonymity in some instances I have changed the names of individuals and places, I may have changed some identifying characteristics and details such as physical properties, occupations and places of residence.

Although the author and publisher have made every effort to ensure that the information in this book was correct at press time, the author and publisher do not assume and hereby disclaim any liability to any party for any loss, damage, or disruption caused by errors or omissions, whether such errors or omissions result from negligence, accident, or any other cause.

Any screenshots that were displayed privately have blacked out names and or faces to preserve privacy, any public set screenshots were left untouched. Fair use allows the screenshots, in contribution to include full understanding of author's responses and points within this work. As well as to include the authors own written words. Fair Use doctrine is also in place since using the source material instead of re-wording all of it into the book helps promote and continue growth and progress of sciences and useful arts. Feminism is a part of social science, women studies, and a huge variety of other topics.

Prologue

Even though some call me a feminazi, no one ever calls me a grammar Nazi. Since I am a poor writer, and I don't have hundreds or thousands to spend on hiring editors, this is pretty much self-edited. I promise I'm trying my best and well aware I suck anyway.

Secondly this weird cross between a book and blog, is something that I can't just lump into a category. I really had no idea what I was going to write when I first started. No outlines. No plans. Now I'm writing this after being nearly done with this book/blog and hoping that abandoning my well planned works, my outlines, and my books of notes will work out.

All previous planned books are… unknown, lame, not cared for, lost to the abyss of internet, never got popular…so maybe the new crazy go at it style will yield results. I'm pretty nervous about having another failure published.

Lastly, many people online and in person really hate me, I'm often called bitch, feminazi, cunt, and worse. Good news is that also a lot people share my views and feels to same, so like, yay and stuff for common ground? By the end of this mess of a book/blog, you may hate me too, or feel happy to have someone relatable. To each their own. I hope you at least can see and expand on perspectives and social issues. Don't take me as a representation of all feminism or feminists, this is after all my own life and my own interactions, struggles, and thoughts.

But if you think I am just a twat you are still welcomed to leave a review, or if you liked it, please, please, begging you, leave a review. Super appreciated. Thank you.

Chapter 1

I'm what some consider to be a feminazi, a bitch, and abrasive personality, a woman who will openly point out the sexism, rape culture, and a woman with opinions. Something many men fear, and many other women even fear as well. [Or just hate.]

I have many names, some are nicknames, some pen names, and some insults but whatever that's life.

I have no real goal or story, this is unfolding as I write and it may lead nowhere or somewhere I have no idea.

I'm in my twenties and fail to see how knowing what I look like will be relevant to whatever unfolds here, but I'm a white woman, blue eyed, average in about everything but many would consider my appearances to be petite, that's just because of the growing American waistband and skinny shaming, not to say fat shaming is okay, really women or men shaming women for having womanly bodies of any kind is moronic.

I will be blunt, I have experienced personally the damage caused by pedophiles, porn, rapists, alcoholics, and abuse.

For the sake of this I probably really should give myself a name, something for you to refer to me as, or bitch will do also, though that lacks class. Crocker, my favorite character from Haven.

From here on out I am the bitch Crocker that is universally hated online by basically everyone because I speak my mind and don't shy away from sexist fuck twats.

So assuming this goes anywhere, I'm going to call this chapter one. Welcome to my drama.

Now how about a history lesson in shit I deal with daily? Well frankly wording it all out will lead me into a million side rants so how about I simply paste in the proof?

Okay was that hard for you to read, if not you need to re-evaluate your ability to spot a troll.

Before I tell you who posted, and why, let's dissect this. Firstly the book was indeed meant for a teenage audience, and in case Americans don't know this, many children, teens, and adults, have rather low reading levels. So yeah the reviewer is correct it was actually written at a lower reading level for the readers. Also the 'lack of description' well many writers don't give you, the reader, every single smell, color, texture, thought, type of fabric, and much more because most people what is commonly known as 'the imagination'. Lastly, yeah spot on there were many grammar errors. BUT. It was a self-published book, no proof reader paid for it [uhm yeah poor writer] and once again go read an actual book they don't always have absolute perfect grammar, and if they did it would in no way mimic how people actually think.

Now for the best part, the main character is a copy of the author, meaning the reviewer knows the author personally and showing the review as a personal attack when calling the author names. Also apparently rape isn't a real thing no random rape has ever happened in the history of ever according to the reviewer.

Here is the punchline the reviewer is an ex stalker of the author, who was denied intimacy and a relationship with the author by the author. Just to clarify, I'm the author.

Not only did a man who stalked me leave this, but that said man is an Officer in Illinois, a member of National Guard, and a now married man- he was engaged during his time stalking me.

Now here is how things went after his review went public.

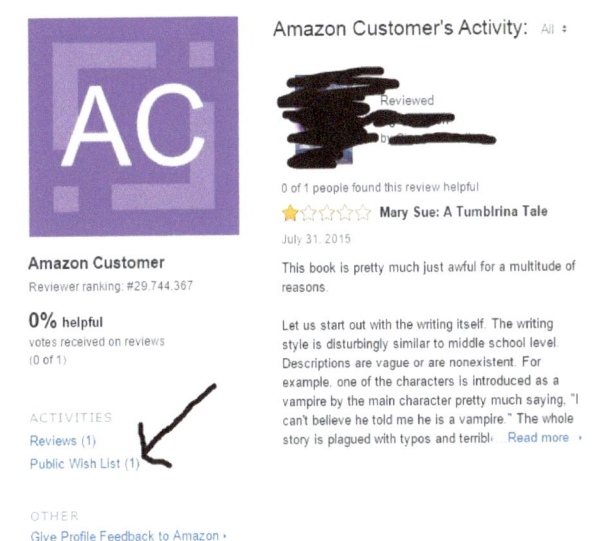

Okay so now you know how I tracked down that it was my stalker who provided that illuminating review.

In case you are wondering why my stalker decided to switch to hate mode like that, I actually saved the messages from when I unfriended him. Sparking such outrage from him;

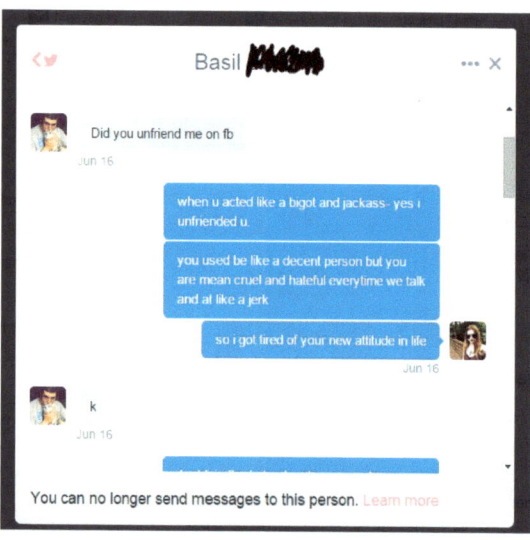

Basil ~~████~~

Did you unfriend me on fb
Jun 16

when u acted like a bigot and jackass- yes i unfriended u.

you used be like a decent person but you are mean cruel and hateful everytime we talk and at like a jerk.

so i got tired of your new attitude in life
Jun 16

k
Jun 16

You can no longer send messages to this person. Learn more

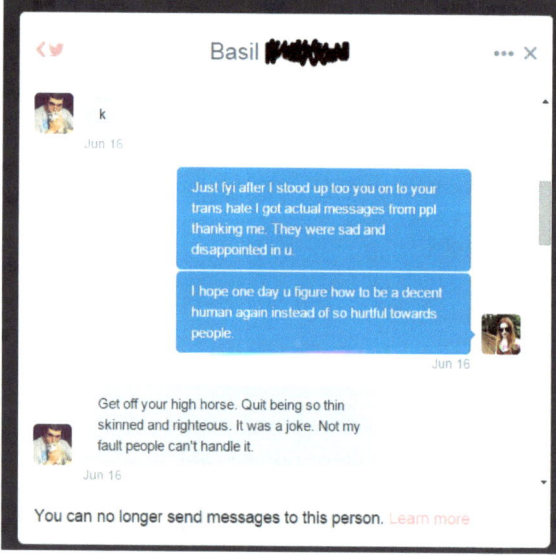

Basil ~~████~~

k
Jun 16

Just fyi after I stood up too you on to your trans hate I got actual messages from ppl thanking me. They were sad and disappointed in u.

I hope one day u figure how to be a decent human again instead of so hurtful towards people.
Jun 16

Get off your high horse. Quit being so thin skinned and righteous. It was a joke. Not my fault people can't handle it.
Jun 16

You can no longer send messages to this person. Learn more

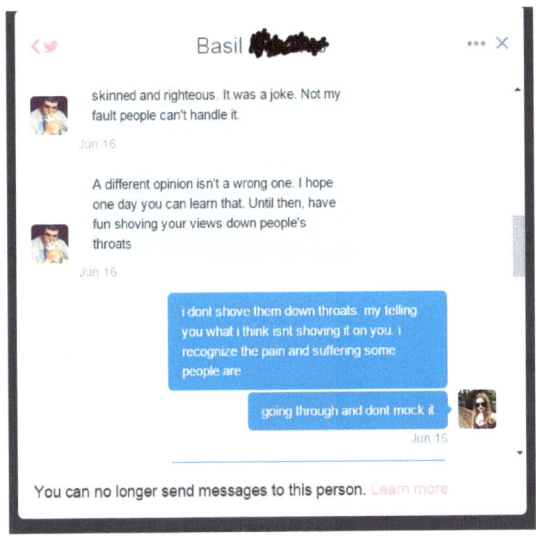

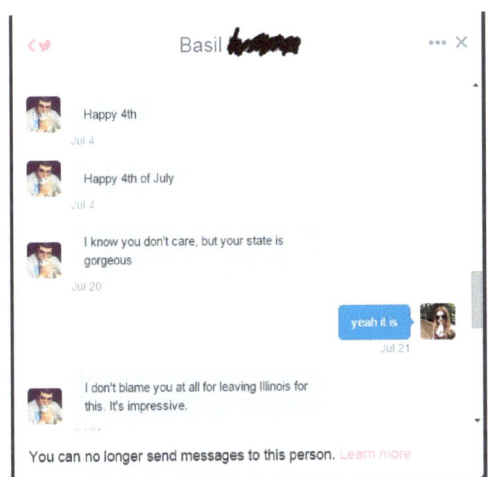

And next to come when I read his review and tracked down that it was him who left it. I confronted him directly about the review.

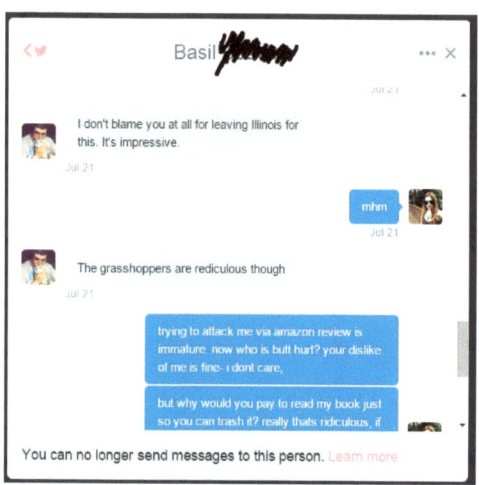

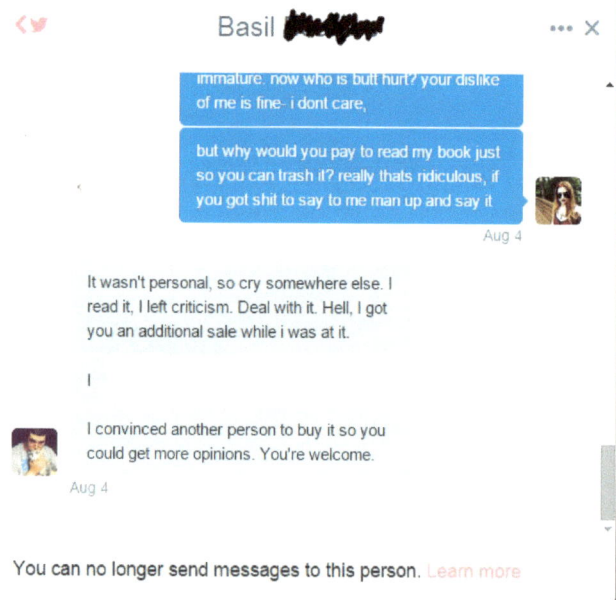

So there is the drama of the review, from a stalker, sexist officer. Also to be clear he did get other people to buy it and then stalk my twitter account and send me tweets for him since I blocked him. To add to this, here are his views of rape culture, and of the multiple sources I left him with for informative information to try and teach him why rape is bad.

Basil ████ ██████ May 23
Internet bloggers seem like whiny babies. Especially video game bloggers. I don't care about your feminist agenda, just talk about the game.

Basil ██████ ███ · Jul 16
What the hell is rape culture?

1:30 PM - 16 Jul 2015 · Details

Basil ███████████ Aug 10
Anyone who thinks buzzfeed is a reliable source for info is a moron.

9:02 PM - 10 Aug 2015 · Details

Yes out of the multiple sources I left him from his question of rape culture, one was from Buzzfeed, but I am a moron apparently.

This is growing long, I actually have about six or seven more screen shots of more conversation from his friend. That he sent to bother me, and more from him, but I will cut this off. As a side note, back before he was a stalker and we were friends- I did hold onto all the letter I received. So Basil, if you read this I want you to know that this, and those letter will happily go to your wife, along with a personal letters from me detailing how I wish her well and that I hope she can courteously stop you from picking up stalking me again. Kindly fuck off

-            The feminazi you hate.

Okay to end this amazing chapter one I will leave you an argument I had today, and to be clear the poster is a womanizer, and I did hear rumors of rape also, who also tried to cheat on his pregnant girlfriend with my boyfriend's ex-roommate. There really is no need to point out which commenter is me after all I am the feminazi right? (Okay I admit I was angry and in rant mode so I wasn't the best rational point maker.)

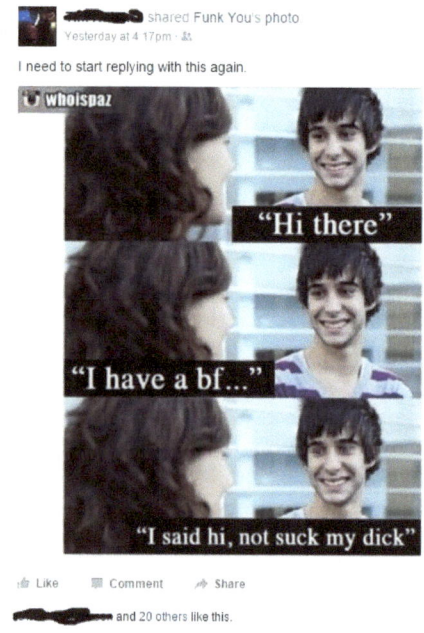

"I said hi, not suck my dick"

👍 Like   💬 Comment   ➡ Share

▓▓▓▓▓▓▓ and 20 others like this.

> ▓▓▓▓▓▓▓ Three times I started a paragraph worthy response to this but all I can sum up is that women who clarify they are not interested in a man is done often for safety of some kind and men should stop being big babies about it. Women deal with sexism creeps and even violent jerks so being upfront is for her own safety. Some stranger a guy likely bigger and stronger than her statistically poses a threat.
> Like · Reply · 23 hrs

> ▓▓▓▓▓▓ I remember moving from Peoria schools to Urbana high. As if it wasn't hard enough to move in hs. I asked some guy where something was and he shouted I have a gf at the top of his lungs and I was like god damn. get it together, I'm just lost, not trying to sex you.
> Like · Reply · 23 hrs

> ▓▓▓▓▓▓ There is a difference between being obnoxious and rude versus clarifying and honest
> Like · Reply · 👍 1 · 23 hrs

> ▓▓▓▓▓▓ Only say hi so people when I want them to suck me off. 😊 so I don't understand his AT ALL. Btw. Hello everyone. 😊
> Like · Reply · 22 hrs

> ▓▓▓▓▓▓ My general response is "ok....cool?" Then continue along with whatever I was intending to converse about.
> Like · Reply · 👍 4 · 21 hrs

> ▓▓▓▓▓▓ , I agree that the is a difference there. I would say that perhaps you should have had that in the with your initial reply. Posting it after ▓▓▓▓▓▓'s reply makes it sound like you were back peddling. after being shown it runs both ways.
> Like · Reply · 7 hrs

---

being shown it runs both ways.
Like · Reply · 7 hrs

> ▓▓▓▓▓▓ Oh bull common sense shows a difference with saying something or screaming it obnoxiously. If others don't have common sense enough to see that difference and post like this two situations are the same then sure I will come back and point it out. It's not back peddling.
> Like · Reply · 7 hrs

> ▓▓▓▓▓▓ People are morons, as a whole. You actually do need toy sleek out things for them, in order to avoid miscommunication. It's was still the impression that was given though.
> Like · Reply · 6 hrs

> ▓▓▓▓▓▓ Your need to undermine valid points with the excuse of not accounting for every idiots misconception is astounding.
> Like · Reply · 6 hrs

> ▓▓▓▓▓▓ I'm actually not trying to undermine you. In fact, I agree with you.
>
> It was the way you presented it that I was questioning, nothing more.
>
> Now, your last reply was bordering upon insulting me. Let's not bait each other into name calling.
> Like · Reply · 5 hrs

> ▓▓▓▓▓▓ I have no problem making my thoughts known, you very much were undermining, saying I was back peddling, despite my message seeming pretty damn clear. I see loads of sexist posts from you, and for once decided to speak up on one of them. no I am not baiting you stating that I often find you to be sexist and rude is simply my opinion of you. I doubt you have any fantastic opinions of me- and you are welcome to think whatever you want. I have been clear in my responses on here, and my points were made. I am not responsible for people being incapable of understanding.
> Like · Reply · 5 hrs

> ▓▓▓▓▓▓ You know, I think that is literally the first time someone has ever referred to me as sexist. I find that interesting. The ruseness is after all part of my puckish charm. I prefer to think of it as crass and curt personally. You're of course entitled to your opinion. In regards to you personally, I have very little

much were undermining, saying I was back pedaling, despite my message seeming pretty damn clear. I see loads of sexist posts from you, and for once decided to speak up on one of them. no I am not baiting you stating that I often find you to be sexist and rude is simply my opinion of you. I doubt you have any fantastic opinions of me- and you are welcome to think whatever you want. I have been clear in my responses on here, and my points were made. I am not responsible for people being incapable of understanding.

Like · Reply · 5 hrs

You know, I think that is literally the first time someone has ever referred to me as sexist. I find that interesting. The ruseness is after all part of my puckish charm. I prefer to think of it as crass and curt personally. You're of course entitled to your opinion. In regards to you personally, I have very little opinion whatsoever.

Like · Reply · 👍 1 · 5 hrs

When a picture highlighting a social faux pas becomes an opportunity to manufacture righteousness. Thank you Facebook.

Like · Reply · 👍 2 · 4 hrs

I know I'm not part of this conversation but i have known you a long time Tim, and I don't find you sexist. Flirtatious but not sexist.

Like · Reply · 👍 2 · 3 hrs

What the hell happened here?? I don't have a clue how this post became about sexism or whatever...I agree with the meme's point. I think assuming a man is nice to you because he wants sexual favors or is going to try to force himself on you is well...sexist.

Like · Reply · 2 hrs

Being a huge dick too a person simply stating they are in a relationship is in itself proof. If a person can state they are in a relationship to avoid possible misunderstanding so that the rest of a conversation can go okay the other person should respect that and move on. If someone is screaming or being a jerk about being taken then yeah that's jerky but literally this meme isn't even a woman being a jerk or mean or anything. Yet haha let's be dicks to a woman trying to avoid possible misunderstanding or harassment. Her reaction wasn't fucking sexist it was just honest and clear but God forbid a woman wants to be sure some stranger isn't gonna harass her.

a long time Tim, and I don't find you sexist. Flirtatious but not sexist.
Like · Reply · 👍2 · 3 hrs

What the hell happened here?? I don't have a clue how this post became about sexism or whatever...I agree with the meme's point. I think assuming a man is nice to you because he wants sexual favors or is going to try to force himself on you is well...sexist.
Like · Reply · 2 hrs

Being a huge dick too a person simply stating they are in a relationship is in itself proof. If a person can state they are in a relationship to avoid possible misunderstanding so that the rest of a conversation can go okay the other person should respect that and move on. If someone is screaming or being a jerk about being taken then yeah that's jerky but literally this meme isn't even a woman being a jerk or mean or anything. Yet haha let's be dicks to a woman trying to avoid possible misunderstanding or harassment. Her reaction wasn't fucking sexist it was just honest and clear but God forbid a woman wants to be sure some stranger isn't gonna harass her
Like · Reply · 1 hr

When someone says hi to me,I say hi back. End of story. If he/she ends up being a jerk after that,then I react appropriately. I'm sorry you misunderstood the intent of my comment,it really wasn't about the meme so much as your overreaction.
Like · Reply · 1 hr

People, you, can think whatever you want of me I don't care. It's all in the situation and frankly some creepy guy just starts talking me yeah I would be clear pretty fast I wasn't available. and people somehow thinking a woman stating her unavailabili... See More
Like · Reply · 1 hr

Actually,I'm a domestic violence survivor,and have quite often been sexually harassed by men,but assuming every man is evil for saying hi is a little quick to passing judgment and kind of bitchy. If you've actually been victimized in the past,you need to heal.
Like · Reply · 👍1 · 1 hr

Chapter 2

Time for upsetting you the readers... again. This is where some of you may hop of the train so to speak. I will post a rant, and then a second rant, from one of my Tumblr pages. Now some of you may have even been inclined after the first chapter to keep giving this a chance but let's face it no one like a woman who mouths off and is often angry. So this chapter will likely piss some of you off. So be it. I was clear as I could be when posting, and if it still offends you, I'm totes not sorry. [This is direct copy and paste I am not even correctly my annoying grammatical or spelling errors]

"The unpopular view of 'white feminism'

First of all, this will piss you off. It will. I promise. So if you keep reading, it is your own messed up decision to allow yourself to get upset.

White feminism the new insult thrown around towards whites who are feminist. The new fad created by waring pop culture stars.

What is feminism? Equality of the genders, usually a way a uniting women and men of various ages, backgrounds, classes, races/ethnicities, for the purpose of creating equality such as equal pay for equal work, fighting and stopping rape culture, promoting healthy activities etc.

So why do I have a big hate for the term white feminist? Simple. Any person who denies that people may experience inequality differently or deny helping certain people based on differences, is just not a feminist. White feminist is a new shitty way of adding a divide and hatred of white women from feminism.

Hating a person for their skin being white is racist- hating a person who experienced inequality different from you is just a shitty thing to do.

Feminists want to understand and help solve those problems, those differences are not a big dividing omg thing, they are an inequality in treatment that should be solved together.

I do not hate African Americans, I accept racism plays a part in how they are treated institutionally, and I know I can't ever understand fully their perspective, but I also know that the negative treatment you receive is shitty and not ok and will fight and continue being a feminist that wants to help and overcome that.

So why the fuck would you take a friendly feminist, see her skin is white and put on the big white feminist hate hat and start dividing feminism into color codes???????????? Yeah there are differences and they can be embraced supported and a continued fight for feminism at its core- equality can keep going. Is it really so damn hard to understand that white feminism is racist and assholian sounding? We don't say black feminism do we? Because feminism is feminism and not feminism is not feminism.

So kindly fuck off with the not feminist bullshit spouting hatred. When you want to embrace differences and support true feminism, please join and fight the good fight, but if you are in feminism to just pick a race war, congrats you undermine the entire movement."

And with that the rant is complete. Something people seem to forget about us, feminists I mean, is that we are human. We like every other human, experience a full range of emotions. We get sad, and angry, and happy, and jealous just as anyone else would. On top of that, despite the frequent overlapping goals of feminism, the means of achieving those goals may be greatly different for various people. That is a tough thing to keep in mind honestly and I sometimes fail at it.

If you can fight past my terrible grammar, the main thought I maybe failed to convey is this; feminists are inclusive and fight for all kinds of women, and saying 'white feminist' is a way to call a non-feminist a feminist by using feminism as the insult. Feminists are feminists, and some pose as feminists but truly aren't. Don't validate fake or mean spirited people by calling them feminists when their behavior is only hateful. Some feminists are still learning and instead of treating them as ignorant scum, choose to educate your feminist allies. So please stop color coding feminism.

I have anger, and it is okay to be a feminist and angry, it is okay to be a feminist and sad or happy or any emotion and it is okay if we take different routes to fight for feminism. I can't always put myself in everyone else's shoes or understand their points of views. Nor can I expect others to be able to do so for me. But the more I type and rant about myself the more I see that may be what I am doing, putting you the reader in a feminists shoes, or at least seeing what it is like for me, that feminism isn't a job to go to but a way of life for me.

I understand haters, and feminists with 'chiller' attitudes may call me a feminazi, but really that term itself is so damn disrespectful of the people who actually dealt with the trauma induced by Nazi's.

Now in case I restored any likability in me, I will post the second rant I posted to Tumblr.

Stop the hair style opinionated BS

Ok I get the insult to some cultures from appropriation but I am fucking tired of hearing white women can't wear braids or dreds or fro their hair or fucking do anything these days. Like really? People think only one hair style per race and region developed throughout all of history? Omg braids never existed anywhere but here and dreads there and short hair styles over there like no. Get the fuck over women doing and trying various hair styles. Clothes sure yeah that can be cultural appropriation but a woman just fucking styling her hair should not fucking matter to anyone. It's a hair style and guess what various styles existed all over the world and being a white woman does not mean she alone can't braid her fucking hair or some shit.

I am a feminist but some feminist blogs I follow are constantly dictating what white women are allowed to do with their hair and that pisses me off so much. What's next? Women can't have short hair ever cuz some group of warriors hundreds of years ago had that? Women can't shave their heads cuz the monks do? Black women can't have straight hair cuz white do? That's all a load of shit. Women can choose how to present and style their bodies without society bullshit trying control them through bullshit appropriation claims.

#culture #appropriation #bullshit #feminism #annoyed #rant #offensive

5 notes   ···

The interesting thing about feminism is that it encompasses so many social issues. Ranging from sexism, wage gaps, rape, porn, culture appropriation, abuse, addictions, and the list goes on and on. Some people will feel more intensely on some issues than others. I honestly have an unusual amount of passion for fighting sexism, rape culture, and abuse. That doesn't mean I don't also have feelings and support for other issues.

Another notion that isn't often brought up is how every feminist is expected to get along with each other by non-feminists or within the feminist movement. Truth is we are human and sometimes people will never like each other and long as you don't dick around and hurt people, that's okay. It's actually okay to not like other people or not share their exact views. I'm a feminist and my personal beliefs and what I fight the most for may be different than many other feminists, and you know what? That's okay, if you are a feminist that does focus on the racial inequalities happening in the world- I don't diss or disagree with you for it. It is good you have a passion and want to make things better. Just don't do it by being a super dick and shitting all over other feminists with different priorities.

I don't expect a lot of feminists to rush to agreement with this book or even show any support of me, in fact I expect hatred, denial, and ignorance. That is the general human way no matter which group a person identifies with. Your possible hatred of me won't stop me though. I will continue writing this book, continue posting online, and continue identifying as a feminist.

If you are still reading this, I hope you know this isn't me speaking for all of feminism nor every feminist. This is my life, my personal fight, and you are reading about an individual (me) experiencing the great big world.

Chapter 3

How do men react to a woman with strong opinions? This is a social experiment we see all the time from women posting how men react on Tinder, Facebook, real life and more. Sometimes results show some dudes are actually pretty great and sometimes they don't. Now I greatly wish I had known I would write this otherwise I would have saved everything back from when I tried online dating...let's just say I met one guy being investigated by the FBI for a child pornography ring and I met a guy who once kidnapped a woman... yeah great prospects right? Thank god I do back ground checks before ever meeting or giving personal info.

I also would have saved every stupid rant I went on, (on every article I notice as eye catching in my news feed). Because wow. I can't tell you the crazy sexist shit that all gets said. Of course if you are a woman you already know.

I do actually have a recent example saved, now you can view the article topic however you want that's not really the point but in case you think context is important, here is a picture of the article that was in my news feed.

This drunk driver killed a teen. Now the teen's parents are going to make both him and his parents pay.

Crash Victim's Family Goes After 'Super Drunk' Driver And His Parents

The family of a Michigan teen...

OPPOSINGVIEWS.COM

👍 Like   💬 Comment   ➤ Share

2,095 people like this.   Top Comments ▾

👍 Like   💬 Comment   ➤ Share

2,095 people like this.   Top Comments ▾

265 shares

Write a comment

Having known alcoholics who came from parents that enabled it...yeah all are responsible. Shitty parenting and shitty kid.
Like · Reply · November 1 at 4:51pm

Bc you know this family?? Once again the police aren't sure if his parents gave it to him and he's 20! How many parents keep beer in the fridge or have a liquor cabinet? Good lord if my parents were to blame for every dumbass decision I made in my 20s.... See More
Like · Reply · November 1 at 6:24pm

Lol you have wrong age plus yeah enabling an alcoholic knowing they are and knowing their actions could kill yeah that's dickish. So sorry you got a bug up your ass but the drunk shithead is an addict and murderer and his parents did nothing to stop him.
Like · Reply · November 1 at 9:00pm

Oswald ▓▓▓▓▓▓▓▓▓▓ You are a stupid fool, you should read the artical, your facts are wrong! You do have a mental problem and should seek help very soon! Your dress is cut very low! So what are you self employed at???????? I'm like you, I'm putting 2 and 2 and 3 and 3 and thinking the oldest profession?????
Like · Reply · November 1 at 10:04pm

Hahaha omg if every low cut dress meant that no woman would be anything but that. Fantastic misogynist sexist logic way to go!
Like · Reply · November 2 at 7:18am

Now if you get past the terrible typing skills of that man, he just insinuated that based upon my low cut shirt* (not dress) and being self-employed, means I am a prostitute. Now also to be clear-that actually isn't the oldest profession. His half assed attempt at an insult was amazingly bad, but still demonstrates the sexism women face online, despite the topic being about alcohol and murder. Despite the load of insults I'm sure a person can come up with relating to actual said topic, he chose to be sexist in his response and focus on my clothing.

I also want to add that even though I appear to be on angry rant mode sometimes, I actually have some normal human moments and make some sense when I type. Another key component of feminism that not everyone understands is that it is inclusive to men and women, along with all other gender identities.

On the next page is a Facebook post that went viral, for various reasons, maybe even you have seen it. (I left this one a little larger to be more readable)

This Woman Drops a Truth Bomb on Bruce 'Caitlyn' Jenner — And This Facebook Letter is Epic!

 Michelle Smith Glass
July 16 at 1:37pm · Edited · 🌐

Dear Caitlin Jenner......being a female, I have never felt brave or courageous or under pressure to pick out my shoes or dress. Courage as a female, is facing your days with a bald head and battle scars from cancer. Courage as a female is carrying a child for 9 mos that you weren't planning on having. Courage as a female is being Mom & Dad to a child while putting food on the table because you are all that child has. Courage as a female is busting your butt to make it in a man's world. Courage as a female is to learn to walk out after you have been beaten by someone who "loves" you. We don't play dress up to feel brave, we are brave in our raw, authentic selves. You will find the most brave women in this world do not dress in the finest fashions adorned by jewels and make-up. They carry crowns of grey hair, wrinkles, tired bodies and weathered hands. Learn the difference. Sincerely, a real woman.

And here is the response I had, and any other true feminists would likely have also [not to mention the LGBTQ community].

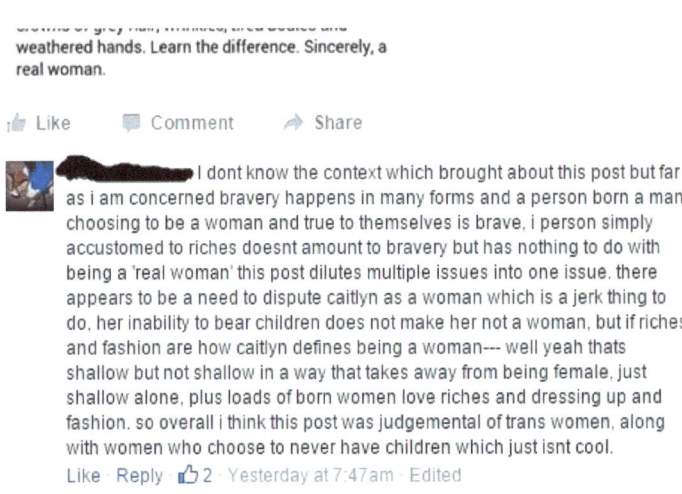

weathered hands. Learn the difference. Sincerely, a real woman.

👍 Like   💬 Comment   ➤ Share

I dont know the context which brought about this post but far as i am concerned bravery happens in many forms and a person born a man choosing to be a woman and true to themselves is brave, i person simply accustomed to riches doesnt amount to bravery but has nothing to do with being a 'real woman' this post dilutes multiple issues into one issue. there appears to be a need to dispute caitlyn as a woman which is a jerk thing to do, her inability to bear children does not make her not a woman, but if riches and fashion are how caitlyn defines being a woman--- well yeah thats shallow but not shallow in a way that takes away from being female, just shallow alone, plus loads of born women love riches and dressing up and fashion. so overall i think this post was judgemental of trans women, along with women who choose to never have children which just isnt cool.

Like · Reply · 👍2 · Yesterday at 7:47am · Edited

Write a reply...

Feminism includes everyone who wants to be a feminist, and often many who don't understand their own views fall under feminism. So I would choose to defend a transwoman. The post that went viral was really just terrible for it also would imply that women who choose or cannot have children are not real woman. I am just repeating my response, a real woman is not one thing. Real women exist in a variety of capacities and different walks in life. Saying any one who identifies as a woman isn't a woman is really just assholian.

Chapter 4

I have woken a good 4-5 hours earlier than I would like, after being up later than I would like. I spent a portion of the night sitting in bed filling out half a post it note pad with ideas for this book.

Firstly, I have no problem dishing dirt on jerks and calling bullshit on the bullshitters. But I would like to add I was not always a feminist, I didn't even hear of it until after high school. So to be fair, I should dish out some personal shit since I call it out on others.

Now when I was in high school things were shitty much like any high schooler will think, but I do recognize then was different from now. It has been a while since I was in school. I am a college graduate, who writes under multiple names, and makes not even a tenth of a living wage. So while I'm not a shining example of leaving high school and moving on to an amazing life, I did learn a great deal of my passion for social justice because of high school.

Now here is some juicy shitty drama about me. For the first three years of high school I had a semi on off relationship with a girl, let's call her Sandra* even though I desperately want to name her real name because she is so evil Hitler would be proud.

Back then Sandra was like a ball of energy and you would get swept into her orbit watching flames burst near you yet never realizing the danger. Sandra was sleeping with married men and breaking up marriages by the time ninth grade hit [yes those men were vile pedo cheating scum bags but I mean she got true giddy joy from breaking a person], Sandra would spread rumors, lie, do drugs, party, she was the stereotypical evil little pot head slut, pardon my usage of slut. See for me a slut is not defined by appearance but by evil actions- such as intentionally breaking up marriages. But moving on, I was too naive to see when she was setting me up. Yep.

Back then cellphones were coming into popularity but still small crap compared to today's phones, on my limited texting plan Sandra used my phone to take 'sexy' pics of me and send them to a guy. Later that night said guy showed up for a booty call with me, and I'm ashamed to say that, to please Sandra, I did indeed sleep with him. Here is the nastiest detail of that, upon kissing me, I learned he had no teeth [meth head] and omg was that nasty and gross, I spent the rest of the time turning my head every which angle to keep his mouth off of me. In the morning I literally kicked him out a window. The window was open and not high up just so you know.

Now at the time I thought I just did Sandra a hot favor of sleeping with a dude and she seemed pleased and cuddled after. Later on when her next target of a man dumped her [apparently my fault- he asked me if any guys were hitting on her and I said yeah because hey they were] but the said guy dumped her and she blamed me.

That is when the truth of the hook up, [my one and only ever] came out. See what actually happened was that Sandra had the number for my best friends crush [I can't even begin to understand how my best friend liked a meth head she could do way better]. Sandra had me sleep with my best friends crush and kept pictures and texts which she sent from my phone, to show my best friend and to end that friend ship.

Oh it ended in a big blow up and after that I spent half of eleventh and rest of twelfth grade with not a single friend in that school. Too be fair there were two other factors to the zero friend's algorithm, which I will add in when it becomes relevant.

This story is something I have partially told people on occasion but I always left out the meth head no teeth part because wow that was nasty, embarrassing, and horrific.

Sandra did many more evil things to me (and others), and current day is married for second or third time. Had a baby senior year, and for some god forsaken reason didn't change her last name to her husband's last name but to my last name when she married. No one else in her life has the same last name as me, and we ended all contact looooong time ago. Now that was some personal information about me.

Chapter 5

Slut shaming. A highly sensitive topic these days. Once again for whatever reason, society thinks of it as a barely dressed woman humping every guy she can, whereas I think of slut as a woman who uses sex and sexuality to harm other people emotionally. If she used sex to harm people physically well the word for that is rape.

Let's go ahead and firstly address the movement and some of its leaders, I am now going to go find some annoying pictures to save to my computer and put here because, if you can't tell, find inserting an image easier than typing every dang thing out.

I'm sick of men being praised for being sexual beings but us women being downed for it.

- Amber Rose

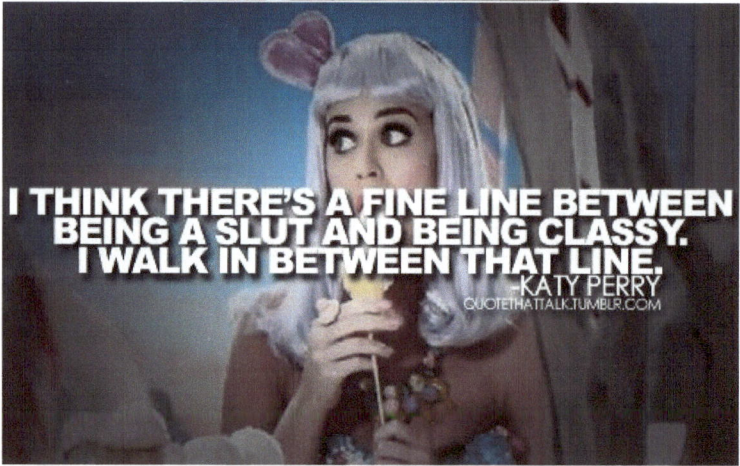

I THINK THERE'S A FINE LINE BETWEEN BEING A SLUT AND BEING CLASSY. I WALK IN BETWEEN THAT LINE. -KATY PERRY

Okay there is some images, Amber Rose is a leading activist in the move against slut shaming while other celebrities add to slut shaming or seem unsure or unaware of the movement, or maybe like me confused by it at times. I'm going to drop in some more images for us all to read and think about then begin my long rant on the movement and how it ties into sexism and rape culture.

I see, so if I don't have sex with you I'm a prude bitch, if I use the pill I'm a slut, if I get pregnant I'm an idiot and if I choose abortion I'm Satan. Yay.

your ecards
someecards.com

I NEED FEMINISM B/C WOMEN ARE SHAMED FOR CARRYING CONDOMS IN THEIR BAGS, WHILE MEN ARE APPLAUDED FOR BEING "WELL PREPARED".

A woman saying yes to a date with a man is literally insane, and ill-advised, and the whole species' existence counts on them doing it.

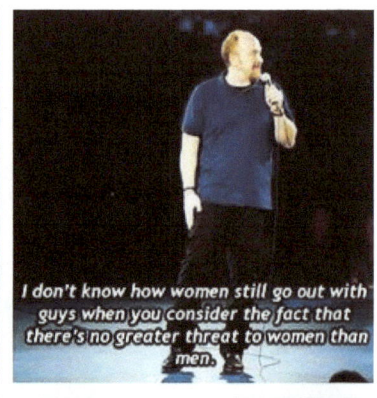

I don't know how women still go out with guys when you consider the fact that there's no greater threat to women than men.

We're the number one threat to women! Globally and historically, we're the number one cause of injury and mayhem to women, we're the worst thing that ever happens to them.

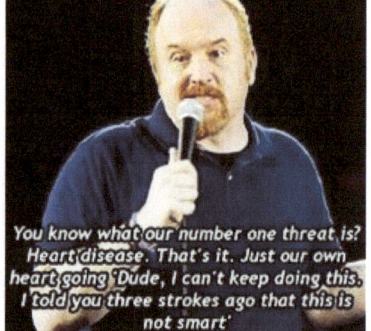

You know what our number one threat is? Heart disease. That's it. Just our own heart going 'Dude, I can't keep doing this. I told you three strokes ago that this is not smart'

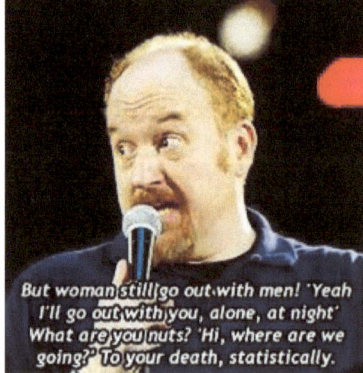

But woman still go out with men! 'Yeah I'll go out with you, alone, at night' What are you nuts? 'Hi, where are we going?' To your death, statistically.

If you're a guy, try to imagine that you could only date a half-bear, half-lion, like, 'Ugh, I hope this one's nice'

IF MALE SUPER HEROES DRESSED LIKE

FEMALE SUPER HEROES

julia
@kickassiani__

"Leave something to the imagination"
I don't get dressed so you can imagine
me naked goodbye

9:16 AM - 29 Nov 2014

Now this is where I may get into trouble I don't have the
original sources to go track down and ask if I may use every one of
these images. Most of this was immediate pop up after a google
search or viral pics that crossed my feed on Facebook or Tumblr. If

anyone knows or is the original poster I hope you are okay with my using the pictures, I didn't edit out any tags or names to be sure posters still get their credit if they did tag their work.

Okay now time to start the rant.

Firstly as a feminist I do and don't understand the anti-slut shaming movement. I do not speak for all feminists nor am I judging those in the movement. I stated before I appear to think of the word slut drastically different than majority of people, for me slut was a term for a woman or man, who sought to cause harm by intimate relations (emotional harm). However I understand from the media that slut is often a term used to insult a woman's clothing choice or her decision to be sexually active, and uhm damn right judging a woman for that stuff is ass-nine.

Woman like Sandra who are out to cause harm are what I would have called a slut in the past, at this stage in life I do try to not use slut in reference to a woman. Women have a right to wear the clothing they decide, and a right to enjoy intimacy, be it in a marriage, relationship, or one nighter- given its safe and not meant to cause harm [aka STD spread].

I would like to add that despite my naïve story of high school, I'm actually conservative when it comes to sexuality and human exploitation. Personally I feel sex is better and safer when repeated with a partner whom understands the need for protection and STD testing, but that is me personally. Many woman enjoy casual sex, and men too, and that is their business.

Here comes my issue with the anti-slut movement however. I see a difference in a woman controlling her sex life and doing what she enjoys, versus sexually objectifying herself and other woman. Meaning a woman who chooses to go have casual sex and is responsible is perfectly fine, but a woman who parades her body in a highly sexual manner and clearly shows herself as being reduced to sexual desire- is objectifying. Yes I see how it can be a fine line.

Woman cry out about men objectifying them often and fuck yeah they do, however there is a responsibility on woman to promote ourselves as people and not a coot for poking when a guy is hard and ready (pardon my language). An example is the disgusting school girl fantasy. Every time a grown ass woman puts on a little school girl uniform she is promoting sexually objectifying underage girls. Putting pedophile like thoughts into a man's mind, just as any man who was into school girl fantasies would be a disgusting pedo in my opinion. As adults do have a responsibility to stop sexually objectifying children and no matter how adult looking a sixteen year old could be, she is a teen and not an appropriate sexual fantasy for an adult.

Now let's hop into the debate of porn, I'm betting you can guess my stance on that. I will say the private photos or videos people choose to make or exchange with sexual partners is their own business and it is never fucking okay to spread that stuff. What is done in private and the confidence of two people or more (whatever), is just that; a personal intimate thing and not okay to ever post revenge porn, share those pictures with your friends, or spread them to any public forum. That betrays a person in some the most terrible ways and these days can earn you a slam of costs and court fees to pay and jail. Don't fucking do it.

Next just so you know the details of my own experiences, yes personal photos have been shared without my permission yes photos have even been taken without my permission.

Third I hate the porn industry not but the act of sharing intimacy with a partner. There are safer ways of becoming intimate rather than the porn industry. Even though there can be bad situations that happen, I think adult chatting sites are in my view okay. Also known as 'camming' (I have done it). I was told by friends that camming would give me a new power over my sexuality and confidence. I hated it. But I get why it can be good for adults. In the comfort of home, doing only what the individual is okay with doing. Meaning if a person gets mean or creepy, block them or log off. [also I view the use of porn or these sites in a relationship to be cheating and a violation of trust unless explicit honesty between the partners and both are okay with said activities, god I can't stress how important it is to be 100% honest with a partner about STDs, porn habits, and if you have multiple partners!]

> ## Porn
> ## is ruining
> ## mens sex lives.
>
> In a survey of nearly 500 college men, results showed the more porn a man watches, the more likely he was to deliberately conjure images of porn during sex to maintain arousal, to have concerns over his own sexual performance and body image and to get less enjoyment from sexually intimate behaviors with a real partner.
>
> EndSexualExploitation.org

Porn perpetuates the rape myths that women enjoy rape & that "no" means "yes."

–Lisa Thompson

EndSexualExploitation.org

MADE WITH FONT CANDY

My hatred of the porn industry does not stem from dislike of sex, it stems from the fact that porn industry exploits men, women, and children, pays for trafficking humans, drugs, abuse, violence, and causes a rampant rise in STDs. Porn teaches young viewers not about sex, consent or treating a woman as an equal partner, but as a hole for his dick. I cannot begin to express how deeply saddening it is that porn is one the all-time huge contributors to a lack of humanity and yet no one wishes to help the victims or support healthier sexual activities and safety.

Porn industry is a global issue. I have had multiple exes with porn addictions, with problems having real intimacy that was harmful or painful for me, who clearly couldn't even be aroused without it, porn does truly destroy lives for those in the industry and those feeding money to the industries pockets. I have read about actual cases of underage boys, some fairly young (pre-teen), raping little girls because they saw their dad's porn and thought it was an okay thing to do. I spent three plus years studying law. There are even cases after mainstream movies such as *50 Shades of Grey* sparking the idea of brutal attacks and rape. The way we portray human sexuality is important. Healthy sex should be taught, safety, respect, health risks, these are the important things to learn.

So yes I'm a feminist who hates porn, sees a lack of distinction between a woman in charge of her sexual life versus objectifying herself in the anti-slut shaming movement. I do support stopping anyone from shaming a person for clothing or enjoying sex. Intimate relations between honest mature adults isn't the problem.

And that is my rant on the slut shaming movement, or whichever appropriate name it should be called and it was combined with my view of what's a huge contributor to the growing rape culture.

As I stated early on, I'm not censoring myself for the readers comfort, I am not toning down my thoughts and opinions, and I do not speak for all of feminism or other women. This is how I am a feminist and how I live my life as a feminist. It is not something I design for everyone else's comfort, nor do I feel I need to be like every other feminist. My intense feeling on rape culture is a huge drive to my feminism and that will never go away.

SAYING PEOPLE WHO ARE OPPOSED TO PORNOGRAPHY ARE "ANTI-SEX" IS LIKE SAYING NUTRITIONISTS ARE "ANTI-FOOD."

About the Author

Well if you do wish to get to know me better, see my other writings, or visit my pages, here are the links;
http://t-crocker.doodlekit.com/
https://www.facebook.com/AuthorCrocker/
http://crocker-t.tumblr.com/

Thank you for reading, please leave a review.